A Day in the Life of a...

School Caretaker

Carol Watson

W
LIN WATTS
LONDON•SYDNEY

Steve is a school caretaker, or janitor. He starts his day at 6 a.m. when he unlocks the front door of the primary school where he works.

Next Steve opens the main gates
of the school to let in Brian and Hilary,
the cleaners. "Good morning," says Hilary.

Steve switches on the heating and checks the boilers are working properly.

Then he cleans and polishes the floors.

4

"Ah, good," says Steve. "The milk has arrived."

At 7.15 a.m. Steve puts some milk in each of the classrooms ready for the children's playtime.

5

Now it's time to unpack the food deliveries.
Steve takes them to the kitchen
for the school cook.

By 8.15 a.m. Mrs Rigby,
the headteacher, has arrived.
"Some of the children's chairs are broken,"
she says. "Could you fix them today
please, Steve?"

Soon the children start arriving.

At 8.50 a.m. the bell rings and they line up in the playground.

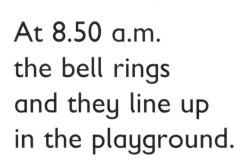

Once all the children are inside,
Steve locks the gate to stop strangers
coming into the school.
"Time for breakfast," he says to himself.

After his break
Steve collects the
letters from the
school mail box.

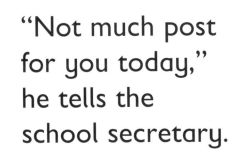

"Not much post
for you today,"
he tells the
school secretary.

Next Steve fills the
paper towel holders.

Then he mends
the chairs.

11

After that Steve tidies the school grounds. First he sweeps up the leaves.

Then he clips the hedge neatly.

"There's a lot of litter around today," thinks Steve.
He uses a spiked stick called a 'litter-picker' to pick up the paper.

13

At 11 a.m. Steve goes off duty.
Now he can have a snack and
rest until he starts work again
later in the day.

At 3 p.m. Steve unlocks the gate of the playground ready for the children's hometime.

Sometimes he offers to help with the after-school sports practice.

At the end of the school day Steve cleans the tables and sinks. "What a mess!" he says to himself.

Then Steve empties the litter bins and tidies the children's belongings.

"There's no name on this," he thinks. "It will have to go into the Lost Property Box."

After that Steve vacuums the carpets, and checks that the doors and windows are shut. Finally he makes sure that all the lights are off.

At 6 p.m. Steve puts on the burglar alarm and locks the school's front door.

"Now it's my hometime," he says.

19

Name check

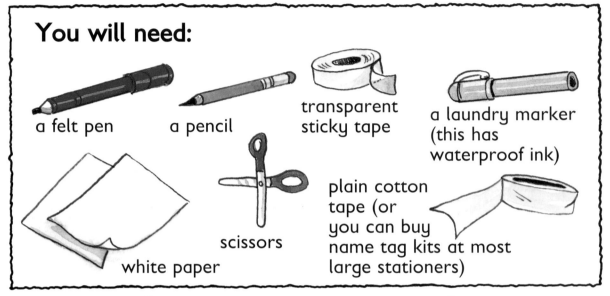

a felt pen a pencil transparent sticky tape a laundry marker (this has waterproof ink)

white paper scissors plain cotton tape (or you can buy name tag kits at most large stationers)

1. Make a list of all the things that you wear to school, or take to school regularly (e.g. lunch box, pencil case, school bag).

2. Collect these things together and see if your name is written clearly in a place that is easy to see. Cross the named things off your list.

3. Make labels for anything that is not named. For plastic or wood things cut out a strip of paper and write your name on it in felt pen. Use transparent sticky tape to stick on the label.

4. You will need a laundry marker and tape to make name tags for your clothes. Ask an adult to sew or iron these on for you.

Do not take anything to school that does not have your name on it. It may get lost.

How you can help your school caretaker

1. Always make sure your belongings are named and do not leave them lying around.

2. Never drop litter; always put it in your pocket or a litter bin.

3. If you are using glue in school, cover the table with newspaper first.

4. Always turn off the tap properly when you have washed your hands.

5. Don't climb on school furniture.

Facts about caretakers

School caretakers have to get up very early in the morning when most other people are fast asleep. They have to get everything in school ready for when the teachers and children arrive. Caretakers have to be good at mending and repairing things and to enjoy working with adults and children.

In order to care for the school and its grounds properly a caretaker has to look out for intruders or burglars. Many school caretakers have their homes in the school grounds so that they can watch over the buildings as much as possible.

When school children are on holiday, the caretaker is still hard at work. This is the time when the school is painted, floors are stripped and polished and many other repair jobs are done.

Index

© 1998 Franklin Watts
This edition 2001

Franklin Watts
96 Leonard Street
London EC2A 4XD

Franklin Watts Australia
56 O'Riordan Street
Alexandria, Sydney, NSW 2015

ISBN 0 7496 4105 3

Dewey Decimal Classification
Number 371

10 9 8 7 6 5 4 3 2 1

Editor: Samantha Armstrong
Design: Kirstie Billingham
Photography: Steve Shott
Illustration: Richard Morgan

With thanks to Steve Brooks and
his family, Mrs Barbara Rigby and
all the staff of Cavendish Primary
School, Chiswick, London.

A CIP catalogue record for this
book is available from the British
Library.

Printed in Malaysia